1000
REASONS
YOU'RE MY
FRIEND

1000 REASONS YOU'RE MY FRIEND

Michael Powell

MQP

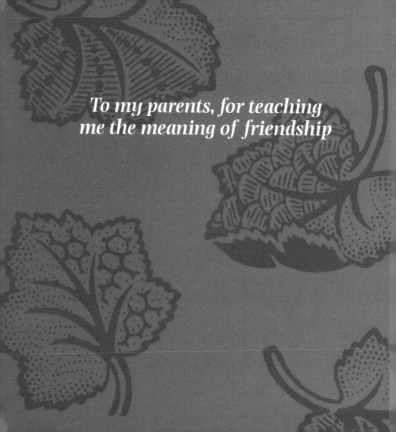

*To my parents, for teaching
me the meaning of friendship*

Contents

Introduction

What is friendship? What is the nature of this special bond that defines our identities, shapes our experiences, and grows stronger with every minute that passes?

Sometimes friendship can seem fraught with contradictions: It is constant and changeable, inviting both curiosity and familiarity; it is challenging and relaxing. It demands honesty, trust, and commitment while offering guidance, inspiration, and delight. It always sustains us through hard times and nourishes us in times of plenty, and it can open a heart faster than a key can open a door.

But what does true friendship really mean?
How does it develop and how does it change?
How do our friends behave and what do they
make us feel?

Within these pages we shall explore all the gifts
that friendship brings and reveal how friends
enrich our lives—helping us to interpret our past,
shape our future, and enjoy living in the moment.

1

What Is Friendship?

Friendship is two snowflakes melting side by side.

Friendship is the sunbeam that pierces the forest canopy to warm the earth.

Friendship is a mystic dance in which we must supply the music.

"It's **not** something you learn in school. But if you **haven't** learned the meaning of friendship, you **really haven't** learned anything."

MUHAMMAD ALI

A friend is someone who gives you the total freedom to reinvent yourself.

Friends never say "You wouldn't understand."

Friendships are sewn one stitch at a time.

Long **before** we are even **ready** or **aware** of it, friendship can **transform** us.

Being someone's friend is a voyage you map out as you go along.

Friendship is God's **special** way of **loving** us through **someone else**.

"Best friend, my well-spring in the wilderness!"

GEORGE ELIOT

Friendship is like a home— it doesn't just happen; it is built and furnished.

You **cannot** collect **all** the beautiful shells on the beach; pick **one** or **two** of the **best** and take them home.

Friendship is the light under heaven's door.

Friendship is a sidewalk in the middle of the fast lane.

The gift that never stops giving— friendship.

Friendship is a ticker-tape parade for two.

Friendship gives a **tiny** clue to what the whole world **could** do.

True friendship is **never** broken, weakened, or strained; it's **simply** tested.

Friendship
should be the
inspiration
for all acts of
creation.

We get the friends that we deserve, and, if we are lucky, a few that we don't.

Friendship can develop in foxholes or in chains; it is a flower that can grow without light or freedom.

a friend takes someone to their destination when they only asked for directions.

Friendship is **both** the **strongest** thing in the world and the **most fragile**.

Friendship makes strangers disappear.

A friend is someone who sees you the way you want to be.

Friendship is the inevitable result of acknowledging that other people matter.

Sometimes friendship is the wind in our sails and sometimes it is the calm waters.

"Friendship is always a sweet responsibility, never an opportunity."

KAHLIL GIBRAN

Love is a sonnet, but friendship can be anything from a limerick to an epic poem.

Memories are the threads that hold the patchwork of friendship together.

Friendship is a **fruit** that is **always** ripe for picking.

A friend is a rare book of which only one copy is made.

Friendship is the art of hooking up to people with no strings attached.

The basis of friendship is simple—trust.

Genuine friends are willing to be there for you; they do not make empty promises.

Friendship speaks softly; it never shouts.

Friendship is an all-terrain vehicle.

"There is a **magnet** in your heart that will **attract** true friends. That magnet is **unselfishness**—thinking of others **first**. When you **learn** to live for others, **they** will live for you."

PARAMAHANSA YOGANANDA

Friendship is caring deeply about someone and making it obvious.

Friendship is not about agreeing but about debating the differences with humor and respect.

Friendship means never holding on to resentful thoughts.

Friendship is a song that everyone can sing.

Friendship is the clothing of God.

Friendship is a safe place from which to take off or to land.

"If a man does not make new acquaintances as he advances through life, he will soon find himself alone. A man should keep his friendships in constant repair."

SAMUEL JOHNSON

If friendship is the **icing** on the cake, it's also the **cake.**

Grapes must grow in sunshine and in rain if you are to enjoy the wine. Friendship is the same.

Friendship is a **game** that everyone **wins** just by **playing.**

Friends can find the common ground, whatever the terrain.

Friendship is a **tool** that must be kept **sharp** if it is to **last** a lifetime.

"True friendship starts by getting to the bottom of yesterday's problems."

CLAUDE ARPI

If you **can't** decide whether someone is your friend, they probably **aren't**.

The **true** value
of **friendship** is
in the friendship
itself.

Friendship is
interdependent
independence.

Some people spend their lives **flitting about** on the **surface** while their friends **swim** quietly **beneath** them.

"In times of **prosperity** friends will be **plenty**; in time of **adversity** not **one** in **twenty**."

ENGLISH PROVERB

Friendship is when you hold all the aces and still allow the other person to win the game.

Friendship is a journey to the center of a circle.

Friendship is the **golden chain** by which society is **bound** together.

When you remove suspicion from a relationship, friendship is all that remains.

"Instead of loving your enemies, treat your friends a little better."

EDGAR WATSON HOWE

Friends come and go as leaves fall from a tree: to allow others to grow in their place.

A friendship is **greater** than the **sum** of its **parts**.

Friendship is the fountain of truth.

Friendship means accepting your responsibilities.

If someone offers you their friendship, put down whatever else you are carrying and approach them with open arms.

Friendship gives you the freedom to choose the moments when you wish to be alone.

Friendship seeks out wise companions.

"Friends should be preferred to kings."

VOLTAIRE

Friendship is a rainbow between two hearts.

Friends are not **made;** they are **recognized.**

Friendship is shared silence.

No one ever destroyed a friendship by listening.

To **be** a friend requires **vigilance** of one's thoughts, words, **and** actions.

Friendship should not be approached with pride, fear, or mistrust, for it is a seed that cannot flourish in a barren heart.

Friendship is staying behind to catch up.

Friendship is about knowing when to say "yes" and "no."

There is **no** effective substitute for **having** a friend or for **being** one.

Friendship is a gift that must be given as well as received.

"True friendship is never serene."

MARIE DE RABUTIN-CHANTAL

Friends give you
an invitation to the
banquet of life.

The true test of friendship
is how far you are
prepared to go to keep it.

Friendship **can** be
spoken **without** words.

Friendship is discovering fragments of yourself in others.

Friendship is the only game where those with the most to lose walk away with the biggest prize.

Friendship is being prepared for **anything** while expecting **nothing**.

To be a friend you must place your happiness in the hands of others.

Friendship **grows** wherever the **seeds** of **trust** are planted.

Friendship begins at home.

"Friendship is Love without his wings!"

LORD BYRON

Friendship is what happens when hearts collide.

Friends are people who **love** the world **through** each other.

Friendship is **giving** someone a **forest** of oak trees when they ask for an **acorn**.

You must spend time carefully gathering wood before you can light a fire. Friendship is the same.

Friendship is a winding mountain path that may not be the quickest way to the summit but guarantees a more comfortable journey.

Friendship lives in our minds but grows through the cracks in our hearts.

Friends are like vitamins: We supplement each other's minimum daily requirements.

Looking for friendship means looking for angels on earth.

Friendship is an **uncut** diamond that must be **shaped** with skill and patience to make it **sparkle**.

Friendship is the difference between breathing and living.

"However rare true love may be, it is less so than true friendship."

FRANÇOIS, DUC DE LA ROCHEFOUCAULD

Friendship is a living thing that lasts because it is nourished with kindness, empathy, and understanding.

Friendship is
the natural result
of following your
interests and helping
others to follow theirs.

Genuine friendship is a
candle that grows **bigger**
the **brighter** it burns.

Each friend is a prayer answered.

Friendship is to **understand** and to be **understood**.

Good friends are the best collectibles.

Friendship is the triumph of the imagination over intelligence.

The bonds that link us together are vital and unique. The name of one of these bonds is friendship.

"Friendship is a sheltering tree."

SAMUEL TAYLOR COLERIDGE

Friendship is one of humankind's most basic needs.

Friendship is the **ability** to **enjoy** the ripples on the surface of a calm lake **without** throwing stones.

Friendship is the **answer** to life's **questions**.

Friends are God's way of taking care of us.

Love is blind, but friendship is clairvoyant.

Friendship is an iron chain that never rusts.

"When you ask God for a gift,
Be thankful if He sends,
Not diamonds, pearls, or riches,
But the love of real true friends."

HELEN STEINER RICE

Friendship is the calm before, during, and after the storm.

Friends are the clues God leaves us so that we can find our way back to him.

Friendship is **warm rain** and **cooling winds**.

Friendship is the fuel that allows common people to achieve uncommon results.

Trends come and go, but friendship has always been the biggest growth area.

You **cannot** make friends with **someone** you have **never** met, but you **can** prepare yourself for the **moment** when you **will**.

Friendship is like a precious ornament that bounces whenever it is dropped.

Friendship is about growing flowers rather than pressing them.

Problems were invented to give friends a purpose.

Friendship is an unusual physical law that states that positives attract.

Friendship is going it alone together.

Friends are messages of faith.

Friendship is not a spectator sport.

Sometimes a friend is all you have and all you need.

2

Honesty
and Trust

"Cultivate solitude and quiet and a few sincere friends, rather than mob merriment, noise, and thousands of nodding acquaintances."

WILLIAM POWELL

I never have to examine your motives.

You **state** the **obvious** when it **needs** to be stated.

Even when you are sure I'll never find out the truth, you won't lie to me.

You would rather hurt me with the truth than mislead me with a lie.

You accept the outcomes of your actions.

You are truthful even when you stand to lose out as a result.

You pay **close** attention to **those** things that **aren't** fighting for your attention.

"Truth springs from argument amongst friends."

DAVID HUME

You return most of the things that you borrow!

When you achieve success you acknowledge those who helped you.

You **recognize** qualities in me that are **invisible** to others— especially to **myself.**

Even if there **isn't** **enough** to go around, you don't mind **waiting** your turn.

You are just the same when nobody is watching.

"If you want an accounting of your worth, count your friends."

MERRY BROWNE

You're not afraid to stand with the minority.

When you do not understand something, you admit it.

You don't care who gets the credit for your achievements.

I **cherish** the fact that you **choose** your thoughts as **carefully** as your words.

To you, elegance is more important than luxury.

You would **never** harm others in order to **satisfy** your **view** of the world.

Nobody can bully you into silence.

You do not **build** your **emotional** life on the **frailties** of **others**.

Right is **more** important to you than **being** right.

I know you will always put things back where you found them.

You don't use my anxieties as a springboard for talking about yourself.

"Friendship consists in **forgetting** what one **gives**, and **remembering** what one **receives**."

ALEXANDRE DUMAS THE YOUNGER

You **try** to
understand the
things that you **fear**.

*We never argue over
unimportant details.*

You **convert** your **convictions**
into your **conduct**.

You make more of yourself available than most.

When you don't like someone, you try to get to know them better.

I **admire** your **unfailing** belief that people's **intentions** in life are basically **good**.

You are **more** concerned with your **character** than your **reputation**.

You are prepared to treat everyone with respect, no matter who they are and whether others think they deserve it.

You don't just stick your neck out for a photo finish.

I am in awe of the way you look the world straight in the face.

You announce your goals and disguise your achievements.

You **never** let your **knowledge** get in the **way** of your **innocence**.

Whenever you get the opportunity to say a kind word, you take it.

"Certain flaws are necessary for the whole. It would seem strange if old friends lacked certain quirks."

JOHANN WOLFGANG VON GOETHE

I would tell you anything, even though you know everything about me already.

At **all times**, you are **gentle** with yourself **and** others.

Whether or not they deserve it, you give people your full attention.

You're **never** so perfect that you **don't** yield to a **little** temptation now and again.

Even when I **know** you're **just** saying something to be kind, I **still** believe what you say!

You judge people from where they are, not from where you are.

When it comes to trust you usually err on the other side of caution.

You command gently and follow with intelligence.

> "Friendship without self-interest is one of the rare and beautiful things of life."
>
> JAMES F. BYRNES

Whatever I have to say, you **never** finish listening **before** I have finished talking.

You recognize the difference between losing your balance and stumbling over the truth.

You refuse to make your mind up about somebody just because they have made their mind up about you.

The beauty in the world unmasks itself to you because you have an open heart.

In an **awkward** situation, you **always** try to put others at their **ease**.

You **believe** that curiosity is **more important** than intelligence.

By refusing to accept anything but the best, you usually get it.

You try to correct your mistakes quickly rather than ignore them.

The **advice** you offer is **always** advice that you are **prepared** to **take** yourself.

"A friend is someone who sees through you and still enjoys the view."

WILMA ASKINAS

Whenever we disagree, you are always the first to say sorry.

While **others** are trying to think up **excuses**, **you** make **promises**.

You seem perfectly content with what you already have.

When you **achieve** something amazing, you're **prepared** to **admit** that **luck** played its **part**.

You always do what you say you'll do.

You can **talk** to **anyone** and **really** connect with them.

You demand to be treated with love and respect.

You **never** let the **sun go down** on your **anger**.

You accept yourself without complaint.

I **never** have to ask you **twice**.

With you it's safe to think out loud.

You don't say,
"I told you so"—
even if you did!

"How often we find ourselves turning our backs on our actual friends, that we may go and meet their ideal cousins."

HENRY DAVID THOREAU

You try to keep your **feet** on the **ground**, in case someone **needs** to **lean** on you.

When someone treats you unfairly, you don't try to get even.

Being kind is **more** important to you than **being** important.

You look for ways to win that don't involve beating others.

You frequently gain the trust of those around you by defending those who are absent.

"Friends aren't jumper cables. You don't throw them into the trunk and pull them out for emergencies."

CHARLIE KRUEGER

When you hug someone, you are never the first to let go.

When **others** are **delighting** in gossip, you **never** get involved.

You are like a tube of toothpaste. You come through in a tight squeeze.

When we **argue**, another gem of **truth** is discovered.

You open your **eyes**, your **heart**, your **mind**, and your **mouth**—in **that** order.

When you are given a compliment, you accept it graciously.

You don't **believe** something **just** because you have been **told** it.

"To find a friend one must close one eye— to keep him, two."

NORMAN DOUGLAS

When, despite my best efforts, I put you in the uncomfortable position of forgiver, you always accept the role.

Whether a person can do everything or nothing for you, you treat them the same.

I **welcome** your criticism because I **know** that you have **genuine** confidence in my **abilities**.

You ask a question and then listen to my reply.

When you say "I'm sorry," you always look me in the eye.

You try to do things the best way rather than just your own way.

While I was trying to keep up with the Joneses, you made them your friends and now they are my friends, too.

You give **more** than you take and take **less** than you need.

The only time you ever go behind my back is to pat it.

You seek respect above popularity.

When I think of honesty and integrity I think of you.

You listen to
what I say and to
what I don't say.

You never resort to gimmicks.

*You don't want it all,
just your share.*

You appreciate beauty for its own sake, not for what you can do with it.

You do **not** speak **because** you **have** all the **answers**. You speak **because** you **have** a **voice**.

You give me what
I deserve, never less.

You never let anyone
else set your standards.
You are always
yourself.

You remind me not to
believe everything I know.

When I get on my high horse, you're never too proud to offer me a ride on your donkey!

When you push me too hard, it's easy to tell you to be more gentle.

"Without wearing any mask we are conscious of, we have a special face for each friend."

OLIVER WENDELL HOLMES

3

You Show Me the Way

"Don't walk in front of me, I may not follow;

don't walk behind me, I may not lead;

walk beside me, and just be my friend."

ALBERT CAMUS

You encourage me to distinguish between sound ideas and ideas that sound good.

I can trust you never to be neutral.

When I'm barking up the wrong tree, you lead me out of the woods.

Thank you for
encouraging me to see
that life is not a race
but a journey.

You are the **stone**
against which I **test**
the **mettle** of
my beliefs.

I've learned to appreciate that **happiness** comes from **within** by following **your** example.

You urge me to break free from routine and follow my dreams.

You think big thoughts and relish small pleasures.

You never use more words than you need.

You offer me impressions rather than opinions.

If something is
inevitable, you do
not waste time
fighting it.

"Never refuse any advance of
friendship, for if nine out of
ten bring you nothing, one
alone may repay you."

MADAME DE TENCIN

I admire the way you never reject an idea just because you don't know enough about it.

You rate performance over potential.

You are prepared to **stand back** and let others **take their turn** as leaders.

When the window of opportunity appears, you don't allow me to pull down the blinds.

You **enrich** the **quality** of **every day.**

You treat life as
a creation rather
than a discovery.

You hatch my chickens before
I even have time to count them.

While **others**
are kicking **back**,
you kick **forward**.

You dare to **begin** and you dare to **quit**.

We may walk slowly together, but never backward.

Sometimes you say **nothing** and it's **just** what I **want** to hear.

"*Nothing makes the earth seem so spacious as to have friends at a distance; they make the latitudes and longitudes.*"

HENRY DAVID THOREAU

You are cautious and yet courageous.

You look for solutions rather than excuses.

I **wish** I could be **like you** because you always **make** more opportunities than you **find**.

You **remind** me that I am **younger today** than I will be **tomorrow**.

I do not mind the shadows, because I know this means you are shining a light somewhere nearby.

People appreciate the way you say "I will" instead of "I'll try."

Even if you have **already** made them, you allow **me** to make my **own** mistakes.

You think with your own mind
and feel with your own heart.

I have **learned** from
you that **playing** is
more important
than **working**.

You do not have a fixed
set of beliefs: You're still
collecting some.

You don't have to make **grand** gestures to show me you **care.** A phone call says it all.

You show me
how to live
without the things
I do not need.

Your **words** bring me to myself,
like a **voice** carried on the wind
calling a child home.

When you run **into** an obstacle, you **never blame** the obstacle.

You take to the open road with lightness of foot and heart and leave it with curiosity.

For you there is
no finish line,
only another place
to start from.

When I go down to the
river of your **heart,**
it is never **dry.**

You remind me that it's never too late to begin.

You **adapt** yourself **cheerfully** to **new** things.

You're never too busy to look me up.

"Sometimes all a person needs is a hand to hold and a heart to understand."

ANDY ROONEY

You listen a **hundred times** before you speak **once**.

Your **securities** far outshine your **insecurities**.

When the writing is on the wall, you knock down the wall.

You never rob me of the opportunity to make a bad choice on my own.

I can rely on you either to
find a way or to make one.

You trust **nature**
to give you **some**
of the **answers**.

The thoughts that escape
from my mouth don't
seem to bother you.

You help me **recognize** when I **have** choices and when I **don't**.

You're **thrilled** by what's around the **next corner**, but you don't **rush** to **reach** it.

Others cross my path but you make me look at the view.

"But every road is rough to me That has no friend to cheer it."

ELIZABETH SHANE

You do not **measure** what is **possible** by what has gone **before.**

When I was inconsolable you did not run away from my sadness.

You never look too far ahead nor too far behind.

Not only do you know **where** you are **going,** but you know **who** you will **share** it with when you **arrive.**

You **never** ask a **question** unless the **answer** makes a **difference**.

I can clearly see how much you enjoy simple pleasures.

When necessary, you have the courage to take big steps.

"A single rose can be my **garden** ... a single friend, my **world**."

LEO BUSCAGLIA

You don't compare yourself with others.

You always adjust your sails to catch the wind.

When I **lack** the **tools,** you **dig** even **deeper**.

You **inspire** me to **find** that something **inside** myself that is **superior** to **circumstance.**

You encourage me
to think "What if?"

You urge me to see
the sense in the world.

*Like the feathers in
an arrow, you help me
to fly straight.*

"The most beautiful discovery true friends make is that they can grow separately without growing apart."

ELIZABETH FOLEY

*At times of darkness,
you scatter light.*

You strive for
excellence instead
of **perfection**.

Instead of waiting for inspiration,
you open new frontiers.

When the **cards** are **stacked** against me, you **reshuffle** the deck and deal **again**.

You paper over my cracks.

The only time you walk away from me is to check if the coast is clear.

I can see **more** clearly when I **climb** up on your **shoulders.**

You always **try** to help me **even** when you're not sure **how** to.

I admire the **way** you view **every** stumbling block as a **stepping**-stone.

It doesn't matter how small my steps are because you keep me heading in the right direction.

"Friendship of the **mind** sees **no** destination. Friendship of the **heart** sees destination **everywhere**."

SRI CHINMOY

You swim upstream with me when everyone else is going with the flow.

Things develop when you're in the picture.

You've taught me that life doesn't have to be a popularity contest.

Without even trying, you have made a big difference in my life.

All other advice is free, but yours is priceless.

You **reach** for my **hand** and **touch** my **heart**.

Walking **with you** in the **dark** is better than walking **alone** in the **sunshine**.

"How rare and wonderful is that flash of a moment when we realize we have discovered a friend."

WILLIAM E. ROTHSCHILD

You **square** things just by being **around**!

You have added colors to my life.

When I come **unstuck**, you **stick** to me.

You share your friends with me.

When it hurts to look **back**, and I'm scared to look **forward**, I suddenly notice you standing **beside** me.

You hear the **song** in my **heart** and **sing** it to me when I **forget** the **tune**.

Friendship is a perfect illustration of how daily miracles appear in the most ordinary of circumstances.

When I need help you never ask if there's anything you can do. You just do it.

You gently **nudge** me if I'm not paying **attention** when **good** things come my way.

"*Each friend represents a world in us, a world possibly not born until they arrive, and it is only by this meeting that a new world is born.*"

ANAÏS NIN

If everyone else in the world walked away I could rely on you to stay.

You are **there** for me **even** when you would **prefer** to be somewhere **else**.

You **show** me the way to turn my **mind** and **body** into instruments of **freedom.**

Friendship is a priceless treasure, never to be bought or sold—it can only be cherished.

I know that you would be willing to give me what I hope I will never have to ask for.

If I **refuse** your support, you are **proud** that I can do it on my **own**.

Even when you don't have all the answers, you ask me the right questions.

When I **lose** my way, you are the **beacon** that **guides** me home.

"Love is only chatter; friends are all that matter."

FRANK GELETT BURGESS

When I stumble,
you pick me up,
dust me off, and get
me moving again.

You **help** me to **free**
myself from **my** opinions,
so I **can** consider the
opinions of **others**.

You **always** find time for **me** when I **can't** find time for **myself**.

It's a jungle out there. Thank you for being my survival kit.

You let me shelter under your wings while I grow my own.

When my spirits are low, you show me something to be thankful for.

You help me to face the unknown, because you have allowed me to see your own fear so that I know I am not alone.

"Friends are people you make a **part** of your life **just** because you **feel** like it. Basically your friends are **not** your friends for any particular **reason**. They are your friends for **no** particular reason."

FREDERICK BUECHNER

The **only** time you **ever** get in my way is to **stop** me from falling.

You made **sacrifices** so that I could **follow** my **dreams.**

When everyone else was jumping on the bandwagon, you offered me a piggyback. Thanks for the ride!

When **everyone else** is thinking **only** of themselves, **you** think of **me**.

You are my safety net when I fall off life's trapeze.

You are prepared to fight your battles more than once in order to win them.

You're the whole nine yards and you'd jump them for me, too.

When you say "I'll catch you later," I know that you **probably** will.

You help me trust my ability to handle whatever comes my way.

Whenever I take a wrong turn, you always wait for me while I retrace my steps.

"Treat your friends as you do your pictures and place them in their best light."

JENNIE JEROME CHURCHILL

The **walls** that I build **around** myself are **no obstacles** to you. You **always** find a way to **scale** them.

When the world is too busy, you help to slow me down.

I am most sure of you on those occasions when I am most unsure of myself.

You are willing to upset the apple cart to find the fruit of compassion.

Instead of waiting for your boat to come in, you swim out to it.

You **share** your **knowledge** and **wisdom** with me, **knowing** that you will **not** be **diminished** when these gifts make me **fly**.

You
Know Me

You can **pick** the **lock** to my **thoughts**.

You never deny my right to grow and seek the truth.

We can make **small talk without** mentioning the **weather**.

"Never **judge** someone by **who** he's in **love** with; judge him by his **friends**. People fall in **love** with the most **appalling** people. Take a **cool, appraising glance** at his **pals**."

CYNTHIA HEIMEL

The **only** time you let me down is when I'm **too** puffed up.

You notice things in me that no one has looked quite far enough to see before.

You love me for my sake,
not for your own.

I like having you
around when I feel
like being myself.

We don't always think the same
but we always think together.

When you see people dancing you try to hear their music.

"No distance of place or lapse of time can lessen the friendship of those who are thoroughly persuaded of each other's worth."

ROBERT SOUTHEY

You make me feel important and you do it sincerely.

I may **wear** a thousand **masks** but you **always** recognize that it's **me** underneath.

You can put a finger on my faults without rubbing them in.

Thanks to you, I have learned that no one is immune from life.

Even if I **fail**, you **admire** me for **attempting** great things.

You **never** assume that the way you **see** things is the way things **are**.

You give me the confidence to change because you accept me just the way I am.

You **never** refuse my **homemade** cakes.

I must have **done** something really **great** to deserve **you**!

You understand yourself in order to understand others.

"Friendship with oneself is all-important because without it one cannot be friends with anybody else in the world."

ELEANOR ROOSEVELT

We honor our differences and enjoy our similarities.

You expect a great deal from me but never ask it.

Instead of moving me around to get a better picture, you tune in to my wavelength.

You do not **consider** that others are **lost** just because they happen to **choose** a **different** route from **you.**

I **know** that you will **always** see me through your **own** eyes rather than **other** people's.

You help me to write my worries on the sand so that they can be carried away by the tide.

My **boredom** has been **cured** by your **curiosity**.

You open my eyes to my own greatness.

I know **you** better than I know **myself**.

When you have **nothing** to **say**, you **say nothing**.

When my dreams turn to dust, you don't complain about the mess.

You encourage me to consider all the options.

"Perhaps the most delightful friendships are those in which there is much agreement, much disputation, and yet more personal liking."

GEORGE ELIOT

Before making yourself understood, you try to understand others.

You have **brought** me **contentment** in place of the **victory** that I used to **seek**.

When words fail me, yours come in very handy.

You **know** what it's like because **you** have been **there** with **me**.

Where others see copper, you see gold in me.

Whether I act upon or ignore your advice, your reaction is always the same.

Even when I am fooling everyone else, you can see the truth and the hurt in me.

Where **others** can see black and white, **you** see **all** the shades of gray.

You accept my limitations and push my limits.

"A **true** friend will **see** you through when others **see** that you **are** through."

LAURENCE J. PETER

Sometimes the best advice you give me is listening.

You have shown me that I'm never too old to dream new dreams.

You **try** to be the **sort** of friend to me that **you** would **like** to **have**.

When I am feeling **bristly**, you **never** give me the **brush–off.**

You don't need an explanation for everything.

You neither look down on me nor keep up with me.

"I have friends in overalls whose friendship I would not swap for the favor of the kings of the world."

THOMAS A. EDISON

I can always rely on you to know how I feel even before I speak.

You don't finish my sentences, but you could.

It's easy to be me with you.

If I want some time alone, you don't get mad.

I can **reveal** my **weaknesses** to you.

We may not be two peas in a pod, but it is our differences that keep our friendship fun.

You believe I'm more special than even I think I am, but you'll tell me when I'm being a fool.

You **know** your own **faults** well enough to **forgive** me **mine.**

You help me to put the past behind me, but you understand when I need to say good-bye to it in my own time.

You can easily sense the needs and feelings of others.

I don't have to tidy the house before you come round.

"Never injure a friend, even in jest."

MARCUS TULLIUS CICERO

You **always** have the **courage** to **tell** me what I need to **hear**.

When I blot my copybook, you tear out the page and burn it to keep us warm.

We have nothing to prove to one another.

You know all my faults and still you manage to like me.

"A **friend** may **well** be **reckoned** the **masterpiece** of Nature."

RALPH WALDO EMERSON

I can make a fool of myself and you'll still be my friend.

I am in **awe** of your **ability** to **watch** the **unseen** and **listen** to the **unheard**.

You help me to think of myself as becoming the person I want to be.

You patiently tolerate
all my questions.

"What is a friend?
A single soul dwelling
in two bodies."

ARISTOTLE

Like a mirror, you reflect
my strengths and swallow
my weaknesses.

You wish me well for my own sake and without envy.

We can disagree and still stay friends.

I am **amazed** that you can **always** put up with my **bad moods**.

The joy of my presence is all you want from me.

Thank you for giving me the freedom to be imperfect.

You always put friendship first.

"Keep a fair-sized **cemetery** in your backyard, in which to **bury** the faults of your friends."

HENRY WARD BEECHER

Before I met you I didn't know what I wanted and I was hurting myself to get it.

It's **fantastic** to know, with **absolute** confidence, that **someone** cares.

You understand my past, believe in my future, and accept me today just the way I am.

You understand the stupid things about me.

Although you are an important part of my life, you don't try to run it.

You accept the differences in others and you don't try to change them.

You **believe** in me even when I **don't** believe in myself. You **trust** me even when I do **not** trust myself. You **give** me hope even when I think I am **beyond** it.

You see more potential in me than I see in myself.

"Friends are not the people you meet at the top; they are the people who were with you at the bottom."

MICHAEL MARINO

Without **asking** for **evidence**, you are **able** to **believe**.

You tolerate my inhibitions and help me to overcome them.

I don't have to act bubbly with you when I'm feeling flat.

I can trust you to tell me things I don't want to tell myself.

Extraordinary things happen when you are around.

When I've cooked my goose, you talk turkey.

"Two persons cannot long be friends if they cannot forgive each other's little failings."

JEAN DE LA BRUYÈRE

You are **more** interested in who **I am** than in who I am **expected** to be.

I **know** you would never **belittle** my ambitions or **laugh** at my dreams.

You help me both to forget myself and to remember who I am.

You **challenge** me **more** than **anyone** I **know**.

I can **always** trust you **not** to make assumptions **about** me.

You **live** your **beliefs** but you never **force** them on others, and **still** they **follow** the **example** you set.

When I am hiding you come looking for me.

"We know our friends by their defects rather than by their merits."

W. SOMERSET MAUGHAM

You always give me your approval, even though you are the one person from whom I do not feel the need to seek it.

Even when you **know** that I am **utterly** wrong, you **stick up** for me.

"Let us be grateful
to people who
make us happy;
they are the
charming gardeners
who make our souls
blossom."

MARCEL PROUST

5

I Need You

One kind word from you can warm a week in winter.

"Some people go to priests; others to poetry; I to my friends."

VIRGINIA WOOLF

Thanks for being here when everyone else was over there.

I used to run
through life so fast
I only saw my goals,

Until you made me
see that God loves
all human souls.

When all's said and done, you've usually done more than you've said.

You **always** give me a lift home **even** if it's **out** of your **way**.

When others bottle it, your support is always on tap.

You're never far at all when I have a close call.

You have **taught** me to **face** my problems **one** at a **time**.

You are my landing lights.

The things that you do take me up a peg or two.

"Friends are born, not made."

HENRY ADAMS

When life hits me below the belt, you help me to get my breath back.

You **believe** that **even** the **point** of **no return** can be a **turning point.**

When the chips are down, you always send out for pizza.

We don't just hang out; we hang together.

You **have** your **say** and **then** you **stay**.

In times of **trouble**, when others bring me formal **gifts** and **flowers**, you bring me a **wink** and a **smile**.

When I am having a difficult journey, talking to you helps me to forget how sore my feet are.

"I have **three** chairs in my house:
one for solitude,
two for friendship,
three for company."

HENRY DAVID THOREAU

The guest book in my heart shows that you have made the most visits.

In a difficult situation you are often the first to drop your barriers in order to find a way through.

I do not love you by what the world says friendship is; I love you only by what I know friendship is.

When I'm **stuck**, you **help** me to **see** the **next** step.

Even when you know I cannot repay you, you lend me your support.

You dispense practical advice, not friendly platitudes.

You **remind** me that there is **always enough** to go round.

I have strength inside of me now, thanks to you.

When I'm driving myself up the wall, you help me down.

You turn a **vicious circle** into a **carousel**.

Friends come and go. Thanks for coming.

You are my eyes when I'm too scared to open mine.

"Don't be dismayed at good-byes. A farewell is necessary before you can meet again. And meeting again, after moments or lifetimes, is certain for those who are friends."

RICHARD BACH

Friends always try to meet in the middle, but you seem to reach me first.

When you **reach** the **summit**, the **first** thing you do is **look down** and **reach** for my hand.

You **give much**
when you have
much to give
and when you have
little to give.

You support me in
my first beginnings
to help me reach my
undiscovered ends.

"A friend is one who incessantly pays us the compliment of expecting from us all the virtues, and who can appreciate them in us."

HENRY DAVID THOREAU

You remind me that life is great the way it is now.

**When the going gets tough
you are more than enough.**

**You are aware of
the treasure of
an ordinary day.**

*For you, success and
failure are never final.*

I don't know **how** you do it; I'm just **glad** that you **do**.

Some people help me to **find** my gifts; you help me to **share** them.

You remind me that nothing is more important than this day.

"Hold a true friend with both your hands."

NIGERIAN PROVERB

I know that you need me as much as I need you.

I can rely on you to keep your head in a crisis.

An apology comes quickly from your heart.

You don't try to solve problems that aren't yours to solve.

You help me pick up the pieces of shattered dreams.

If you **need** my help, you're **never** too proud to **ask** for it.

"The world is round so that friendship may encircle it."

PIERRE TEILHARD DE CHARDIN

Loneliness doesn't get a look in when you're looking out for me.

You can lift even the heaviest of hearts.

Without you **everything** in my life would seem **smaller**— **except** my phone bill.

You **think actively** and **act thoughtfully.**

The climb is less severe if you are near.

"A true friend is the greatest of all blessings."

FRANÇOIS, DUC DE LA ROCHEFOUCAULD

I know I can always turn to you when I've popped all my bubble wrap.

You are **more** interested in **promoting** **goodwill** than in **being** **successful.**

I like the way you stop and think.

A friend **fills** a place that was left **open**.

You're far out and close by at the same time.

You don't mind driving me to the airport.

When I **give** you a **thousand** reasons why I **can't**, you give me the **one** reason why **I can**.

You look for **optimal** solutions, not **perfect** ones.

I know that you would never give up on anybody.

When we are chatting on-line, you don't mind that I'm a slow typist.

When you **leave** I miss the **noise.**

When I'm feeling unbalanced you tip the scales of life in my favor.

Although we may disagree, we never have to start all over again.

If I could have one of your qualities it would be your enthusiasm.

You **search** for that **something extra** that can **improve** things.

You know **when** to **stand up** and **speak** and **when** to **sit down** and **listen**.

The **only** time you put me **down** is when you're **too tired** to carry me anymore.

I hope **one day** you can **lean on me** as much as I have **leaned on you**.

You never let me hang up in despair.

"Friendship ought to be a gratuitous joy, like the joys afforded by art, or life."

SIMONE WEIL

I need **you** to remind **me** that sometimes I'm **ahead**, sometimes I'm **behind**.

You always manage to turn a loss into a new discovery.

You **know** when to **hug** me and **tell** me that it's **going** to be **okay**.

When I talk to you I hear the word "could" instead of "must" and "should."

"The meeting of two personalities is like the contact of two chemical substances; if there is any reaction, both are transformed."

CARL JUNG

When I am at my lowest ebb, you help me to turn the tide.

You **instinctively** know what I **miss** and what I **long for.**

I treasure **all** of the **little** things you **do** for me **without** needing a **reason.**

Your eyes are calm and your mind is peaceful.

"Stay is a charming word in a friend's vocabulary."

LOUISA MAY ALCOTT

You are led by your values, not your circumstances.

You replace "maybe tomorrow" with "here I am."

I **know** you will **always** have **chocolate.**

It's not that I can't live without you; it's just that I don't want to.

You always leave a light on in your heart.

"It is not so much our friends' help that helps us as the confident knowledge that they will help us."

EPICURUS

You tolerate everything except intolerance.

Wherever we go we take a little of each other with us.

Even **though** we both **change**, our friendship **stays** the **same**.

Our friendship **doesn't** make the world go **round**, but it makes the **ride worthwhile.**

If I ask for time alone, you always know exactly when to come back.

I rely on you to show me who I am and where I want to go.

If I were to plant a seed every time I think of you, I could walk forever in a sea of green.

"My friends have made the story of my life. In a thousand ways they have turned my limitations into beautiful privileges, and enabled me to walk serene and happy in the shadow cast by my deprivation."

HELEN KELLER

You **force** me to **clear** out my **clutter**.

When I won't budge,
you give me a gentle nudge.

You always **look**
before I **leap**.

Even **when** we are walking in **opposite** directions we **remain side by side.**

Rather than pretending you know them already, you set out to find the answers.

Your **loyalty** asks for **no reward** but that our **friendship** should **continue** to **grow**.

Some people live in a dream world and others face reality, but with your help we can turn one into the other.

You always reply to my e-mails.

You're all talk—pep talk.

"The best time to make friends is before you need them."

ETHEL BARRYMORE

You help me to listen to my inner voice.

With you beside me I am willing to explore life outside my comfort zone.

When my heart has been broken, you teach me to trust again.

First you **grabbed** my **attention**, and then you **shared** some of your most **precious** secrets.

You **surprise** me with **little** sweet acts of **kindness**.

"No man can be happy without a friend, nor be sure of his friend till he is unhappy."

THOMAS FULLER

You have **many** interests; **some** of them have **now** become **my** passions.

You **blow** the **winds** of **change** in my **direction**.

You always share your happiness with me.

When I need to **blow off** some **steam** you're my **safety valve.**

You never have to pencil me in.

I never have to mind my p's and q's, just *U* and *I.*

You help me to become the person I couldn't be without you.

We are cut from the same cloth, you and me; that's why you can patch me up.

I am not **afraid** of **storms** when we **sail** our **ship** together.

You allow me
the freedom to change
because you have
watched me changing
and growing for so long.

You help me transform
loneliness into solitude.

"Friendship is the
first and basic
human conviction."

DR. WILLIAM S. SADLER

What you **have** you **give**,
instead of **wishing** you
had **more** to give.

The **circle** of your **compassion** grows **wider** every day.

You protect me with your prayers, magnify me with your love, and refresh me with your laughter.

"If you have **one** true friend you have **more** than your share."

THOMAS FULLER

You give me
sixty minutes in
my hour of need.

I can always rely on you to go out of your way to make another's day.

I can **always** depend on **you** to depend on **me**.

On life's journey I often turn around and congratulate myself **on the path** I have taken. But when I look back at our friendship, though the **winds of time** have erased our steps, I am reminded that together we have created something more important than **mere footprints**.

6

Laughter
and Tears

"In the **sweetness** of **friendship** let there be **laughter**, for in the **dew** of little things the **heart** finds its **morning** and is **refreshed**."

JAMES ALLEN

We've shared many **smiles** and many **tears**, but nothing **beats** the **laughter**.

You're absolutely determined to enjoy whatever you are doing.

I can phone you when I have nothing to say.

When you see me without a smile, you give me one of yours.

You **entertain** me rather than try to **improve** me and **usually** end up doing **both**.

Some people grab life by the throat; you tickle it under the chin.

There's **nothing** as **much** fun as doing **nothing much** with you.

You focus on what you have rather than what you have lost.

"It seems to me that trying to live without friends is like milking a bear to get cream for your coffee. It is a whole lot of trouble, and then not worth much after you get it."

ZORA NEALE HURSTON

Whenever you are on thin ice,
you start to dance.

**You take each day
and make it better.**

*You take big bites out
of your slice of life.*

**You have the courage to
make a fool of yourself.**

Even when we don't know where we're heading, we end up laughing somewhere.

You **recognize** that your body can be a **dance hall** as well as a **temple.**

I love the way
you wave at children
on school buses.

You second
my emotions and
lighten the load.

You are generous to
yourself as well
as to others.

The only thing you don't care about is who you smile at.

You are **mature** enough to **revel** in **moments** of **immaturity**.

Your eyes shine with sparkling contradictions.

We may **make** mistakes **together**, but it's **fun** all the **same.**

When I ask you a dumb question I can rely on you to give me a dumb answer.

You're charming, witty, good-looking, and intelligent. We're so alike!

"We are not friends for the laughs we spend, but the tears we save."

NIKKI GIOVANNI

Friends turn a **meal** into a **feast** and a **house** into a **home.**

You're silly at the right moments.

You've got your head screwed on, even though you are a little twisted!

Embarrassing me in front of my parents—just one more service you offer!

You **encourage** me to take things **less seriously**; after all, they're **only** things.

You try to mix a little foolishness in with your serious plans.

I admire your perseverance.

You make every day a friendship day.

Whenever I'm at a **loose end**, I know that you won't be too **tied up** to talk.

"We cherish our friends not for their ability to amuse us, but for our ability to amuse them."

EVELYN WAUGH

In the most formal of situations, you manage to remain appropriately informal.

I ate all the chocolate and you forgave me.

Everything that happens in your life you try to love, and you laugh at anything you can't.

Your **intelligence**
and **wisdom**
are demonstrated by
your continued
cheerfulness.

By never trying to be
noticed you never quite
manage to be ignored.

I cherish your ability to make your own happiness.

"The greatest healing therapy is friendship and love."

HUBERT H. HUMPHREY

You **laugh** at my **jokes** even when they are **not** very funny and **listen** to my **problems** even when they are **not** very **serious**.

You treat me like one of the family, but I forgive you!

You set out to do something silly every day.

You **dare** me to be **myself** and then have a good **laugh** at my **insanity**!

If I had a dollar for every time you've helped me out, I could pay back that money you lent me!

You never let other people's laughter shape your experiences.

Friends like you can't be bought—but they can be bribed with ice cream!

*What a sense of humor!
It's just like mine!*

You cook with reckless abandon.

"The greatest sweetener of human life is Friendship."

JOSEPH ADDISON

You are never **SO** busy questioning things that you **can't** laugh at them.

Whenever I feel crumpled you straighten me out.

You **seriously** believe that **nothing** should be taken **too** seriously.

While others judge me by what I have already done, you remind me of what I am capable of doing.

Your laugh can turn a fiasco into a fiesta.

"We are **friends** and I do **like** to **pass** the **day** with you in **serious** and **inconsequential** **chatter**."

JEANETTE WINTERSON

The door to your heart is always open.

Our jokes just keep on coming.

You'll listen to my music.

You are **worth** your **weight** in chocolate chip cookies!

When I borrow your car, you never stand in my way.

You're **mellow**, like a good bottle of **wine**, and **fun** when you're **uncorked!**

I can always depend on you to double my joy and halve my sorrow.

"The language of friendship is not words but meanings."

HENRY DAVID THOREAU

When we are **together** we **cry** with **laughter** at things that **aren't** even **funny**.

You dance with me in the sunlight and walk with me in the shadows.

*If I could reach up
and hold a star for every
time you made me laugh,
the entire evening sky
would be in the palm
of my hand.*

**We are tied together by
memories, tears, laughter,
and smiles.**

"Thy friendship oft has made my heart to ache; Do be my enemy — for friendship's sake."

WILLIAM BLAKE

You are the **happiest** person I **know** because you **don't** try to be **happier** than everyone else.

There is **nothing** I wouldn't do for you, and there is **nothing** you wouldn't do for me.

How can I be sad? You look so silly when you try to cheer me up!

You sympathize with my strength, not my weakness.

Whenever life becomes bizarre, I look for you and there you are.

When my **heart** has been **broken** and all my **hopes** have run **away**, you **mend** it and then **fill** it up again with **laughter**.

Your sense of fun is a horizon that expands every time I approach it.

You listen to my heart.

You're different, and I'd really miss you if you weren't there.

You have frequent attacks of smiling.

You're not embarrassed when I make a fool of myself.

We can make harmless fun of each other.

"It is a sweet thing,
    friendship, a dear balm,
A happy and auspicious
    bird of calm ..."

PERCY BYSSHE SHELLEY

You **ignite** the
spark of **humor** in
every situation.

You encourage me to
hit the **high** notes.

"Friendship is
certainly the finest
balm for the pangs
of disappointed
love."

JANE AUSTEN

When I **suffered** a great **loss** you didn't know **what** to say, but instead of walking **away**, you simply **helped** me to **cry**.

When I struggle you give me a huggle.

Whenever I ask "Why did this happen to me?" you remind me to ask the same of all the joy that comes my way.

You **keep** me **young** even though you **never** stop **reminding** me about how **old** I am **getting!**

"Sometimes our light goes out but is blown into flame by another human being. Each of us owes deepest thanks to those who have rekindled this light."

ALBERT SCHWEITZER

When all the trees were bare, you spoke of the future when we would pick the fruit together.

You often laugh at yourself and invite others to join in.

Our **shared laughter** makes my head **reel** with **exuberance.**

Whenever my life is going through a dry spell, you point out the high-water mark.

You never feel sorry for yourself.

"When people care for you and cry for you, they can straighten out your soul."

LANGSTON HUGHES

If **listening** is an **art**, you have a **natural talent** for it.

My heart dances because of you.

You fly because you take yourself lightly.

When it's **time** to **face** the **music**, you **help** me to **play** a **different** tune.

"**Have no friends not equal to yourself.**"

CONFUCIUS

7

You
Inspire Me

"My friend, if I could give you one thing, I would wish for you the ability to see yourself as others see you. Then you would realize what a truly special person you are."

B. A. BILLINGSLY

You've taught me it's never too late to start again.

You are
comfortable
with **success.**

The **breadth** of your
gifts is matched **only** by
the **depth** of your **soul.**

To be a better friend
it's plain to see,
I must be more like you
and less like me.

When my
imagination feels
cooped up, you
give it **free rein**.

However **bad** things get, you always have **faith** that they will get **better**.

You have a uniqueness that makes people look and pay more attention.

You don't just make impressions; you leave them, too.

"You can make more friends in two months by becoming interested in other people than you can in two years by trying to get other people interested in you."

DALE CARNEGIE

When life isn't offering a game worth playing, you invent a new one.

When you have to **jump through hoops** just to get through the **day**, you **still** seem to have **lots** of energy **left over**.

While others ponder, you ask, ask, ask.

You **don't** allow the **unknown** to **affect** you.

In the University of Life you earn top honors.

"If you are successful,
you may win
false friends and
true enemies.
Succeed anyway."

MOTHER TERESA

When I'm
broken down, you
show me your **soul**.

I admire your self-discipline.

You gain the respect of intelligent and sensitive people.

Instead of **waiting** for **other** people to be **friendly**, you **show** them **how**.

Rather than saving it for later, you spend your life now.

To you the present is a gift.

You are not unpredictable; neither are you predictable.

You **pay** for your **wonderful** gifts by **using** them.

"You never lose by loving. You always lose by holding back."

BARBARA DEANGELIS

You **go** with
the **flow**, but
you're **not** afraid
to cause a **stir**.

I admire your ability to
enjoy your own
company.

You draw joy toward you without even realizing you're doing it.

You do not seek **happiness** but **euphoria.**

What you can give is more important to you than what you can get.

You have a clear idea of what you want to achieve.

You admire rather than envy.

Win or **lose**, you do it with **grace** and **humor**.

You keep
reaching out
for things that are
just **beyond**
your **reach**.

Whenever you receive
applause, you look
genuinely surprised.

You don't count on anybody else to relieve your stress.

"Everyone has a gift for something, even if it is the gift of being a good friend."

MARIAN ANDERSON

When seeking **different** results you **change** your behavior **first**.

When others can only dream, you take action.

You **maximize** your **potential** by **sharing** it with **others**.

I try to **follow** your **example** by **never** taking **anything** for **granted**.

You don't blame your parents but instead thank them for having you.

I am **inspired** to write words in **praise** of you.

"When a friend speaks to me, whatever he says is interesting."

JEAN RENOIR

Until you've given everything, you won't give up.

You don't worry about knowing people; you just make yourself worth knowing.

You do not allow your doubts to discourage you.

The fact that you can't do everything doesn't seem to stop you from trying anything.

Even when you **only** have a **few** of the pieces, you **try** to **make** pictures.

Most of the **high** spots in my **life** have come about through **your** encouragement.

Every day you challenge me to be happy.

You are never boring.

"Though friendship is not quick to burn, it is explosive stuff."

MAY SARTON

You **insist** on **making** your **contribution** to the **world**.

Once you have found your peace, you pass it on.

You
empower
others with the
strength of
your **beliefs.**

*I'm sure you
change the world
by your example.*

You **bite** off **more** than you can **chew** and **then** you **chew** it.

Whatever the **burden**, you exhibit **grace** under **pressure**.

You're my sixth sense.

*You're the skip
in my step.*

**You're the coins
in my fountain.**

**You are my
dream catcher.**

"A friend is someone who, upon seeing another friend in immense pain, would rather be the one experiencing the pain than watch their friend suffer."

AMANDA GIER

To you, change is more crucial than results.

Your **presence** is a **present** to the **world**.

However little you have, you are still generous with your time.

Sometimes you make me feel irreplaceable.

I find your enthusiasm **contagious**; you could start an **epidemic**.

*Every day of your life
you scatter creative seeds.*

**When others
can't see the target,
you aim straight for
the center.**

You don't wait for other people's
permission to live your life.

You **luxuriate** in the **space between** where you **are** and where you **want to be**.

"My friend is that one whom I can associate with my **choicest** thought."

HENRY DAVID THOREAU

You never
let yesterday's
disappointments
overshadow
tomorrow's dreams.

Life is **tough**,
but you're **tougher**.

You color
outside the lines.

*You don't get hung up
on the little things.*

You **accept** insults graciously, by **ignoring** them.

You **find** the good in **everything**, because you **look** for it.

When the world is going bananas you don't go ape.

If you have something you **don't** need, you give it to someone who **does.**

"One loyal friend
is worth
ten thousand
relatives."

EURIPIDES

Every day, you seek to expand your freedom a little bit more.

Although you believe in miracles, you don't depend on them.

You do so much for so many people who never realize it.

Although you **ask** for a **lot**, you **take** what is **offered**.

My **friend**, you **light** up my **life** every **single** day.

You never confuse a single defeat with an ultimate defeat.

You have confidence in the truth, although you may not always be able to comprehend it.

You are **prepared** to say **no** to **many** things to **leave** you **free** to say **yes** at the most **important** moments.

I'm the first person you call if you've got a good idea.

It's **impossible** for you to **hide** your **beautiful** soul.

You act and leave the talking to the others.

"A friend is a present you give to yourself."

ROBERT LOUIS STEVENSON

You live your life as if everything is a miracle, and you encourage me to see beauty in the world.

You **open** your arms to **change**, but you **never** let go of your **values**.

Being in your company
elevates me.

Because of you,
I **believe** there
really is **good**
in the world.

I admire the light
that's inside of you.

When I am reaching for the stars, you remind me of the flowers at my feet.

You **help me** to **pursue** what I **want** rather than **settle** for what is **comfortable.**

You **never** try to **stop** the **rain** by **complaining**.

"**Plant a seed
of friendship;
reap a bouquet
of happiness.**"

LOIS L. KAUFMAN

You **never** seem to **waste** energy by **worrying**.

If it is for the benefit of others, you're not afraid to break the rules.

You never assume that your beliefs and expectations are shared by everybody else.

I've **learned** from **you** to do **ordinary** things in an **extraordinary** way.

You are charming, but you don't rely on it.

Whatever people **expect**, you always give **more**.

The only person you try to outstrip is yourself.

I admire your ingenuity.

You rise above the mediocrity of your surroundings.

You believe in a world of peace and you try to spread it wherever you go.

Friendship **gives** me the **courage** to lose **sight** of the **shore** in my **search** for new **lands**.

"Without friends no one would choose to live."

ARISTOTLE

You do your best and then wait patiently for the results.

Before you think, you always dream a little.

You always try to make a difference.

To you everything is a worthwhile experience.

You're a **realist** who **believes** in **miracles**.

Each day
you try to learn
something new.

You **live** your **life**
hoping to **find**
adventure while others
secretly hope that
they **won't**.

You are the **pearl**
that has **taught** me
that all the **world**
is my **oyster**.

How do you manage to be
in the midst of trouble and
still be calm in your heart?

Your **energy** is **boundless,** your **honesty** is **unwavering,** and your **faith** in **me** is **indestructible.**

"Every gift from a friend is a wish for your happiness."

RICHARD BACH

Yesterday's **defeats** never cause you to **complain**.

You are the most necessary person I know.

You are **motivated** by your **loves** and **not** your **hates**.

Like a **rainbow**, you **brighten** my **life** when I have been **through** a **storm**.

Sometimes you hold my hand, but you always hold my attention.

You take **pleasure** in the **simplest** things— **even me!**

Whatever I should do, you make sure I do it.

Your imagination guides you.

You act spontaneously rather than on your fears.

If you were a flower, you'd be a forget-me-not.

You take the cake—and work out the recipe later.

Regardless of the circumstances, you do what needs to be done.

When in doubt you're an optimist.

You **have** the **curiosity** of a **child.**

You take time to wonder.

I didn't
think orange
went with purple
until you showed
me a sunset.

8

Friends
Are Forever

"Friends are like melons.
Shall I tell you why?
To find one good
you must a hundred try."

CLAUDE MERMET

It's **you** and **me** against the **world**, so this is your **last** chance to **switch** teams.

There are **acquaintances**, **friends**, and **best friends**—and **then** there is **you**.

You **hold** your head **high**, but **always** at a **friendly** level.

You're my lead violin.

Without you where would I begin?

You **remind** me of **someone I see** when I **stare** into a **calm** lake.

You are my endless sky.

I **know** you **choose** your friends **carefully—thanks** for **choosing me.**

It has taken a short time to know you, but it would take me a lifetime to forget.

"A brother may not be a friend, but a friend will always be a brother."

SAMUEL RICHARDSON

You are my dream team of one.

Our friendship is going to be the stuff of legends.

You are **always** worth the **trouble** and I **know** you'll **never** give up on me.

If I had to live my life again, I'd like to meet you sooner.

With your score, the best of the rest don't pass the friendship test.

You are someone I hope to stay young with while I grow old.

Most things cease to be **wonderful** when you get used to them, but our friendship just keeps getting **better**.

We may not always
see eye to eye,
but we never stop
looking.

I'm having the
time of your life.

Nobody will ever build a statue dedicated to you, but the music of your life will play on in the hearts of your friends.

"Good company in a journey makes the way seem shorter."

IZAAK WALTON

You **play** the friendship **game** for **keeps**.

You planted a tree on my birthday.

Right now we are **making** some **great** memories **together**.

I **know** the future will be a **better** place if **you** are there.

A **musician** must **compose** music; a **poet** must **write** poems; **you** must **make** friends.

You are my place in the sun.

The **future** can **wait**, so **long** as we're **together**.

You **leave** the **best** bits for **me**.

"Then come the wild weather, come sleet or come snow,

We will stand by each other, however it blow."

SIMON DACH

Chance made us **meet;** **time** made us **friends.**

You last longer than the tough times.

We are made from the **same mold**, just filled with **different stuff.**

Instead of looking for friends who are like me, now I look for friends who are like you.

Thank you for **never** bragging about your **success** or your **plans**.

You **make up** for some of the **qualities** that I feel I **lack**—but **don't** ask me **which ones!**

When **times** are **hard**, you **keep** your **heart soft.**

You can still remember
my favorite poem.

*When something
matters to me, it
matters to you, too.*

You recognize that words
last longer than temples.

Our friendship is like freshly fallen snow. It bestows an extraordinary kind of silent beauty on ordinary things.

Time spent with you
is never long enough.

**If friends were
flowers, I'd still
pick you.**

You are like a movie I
can watch over and over.

"The ornament of a house is the friends who frequent it."

RALPH WALDO EMERSON

It's **not** that we **disagree**; it's **how** we **disagree** that **makes** us **last**.

You **show** up, **stand** up, **open** up, **put** up, and **make** up with me.

I think I have finally found my place in this world—next to you.

Friendship is not **something** you **seek**, it is **something** you **build**.

If life is a dream, then I'm really glad you're in mine.

Life may be an illusion, but you seem pretty real to me.

We are **all** given **gifts**, but it **looks** like you've **opened** yours **first**.

On the **road** of **life**, you're by **far** the best **diversion**.

"Never shall I forget the times I spent with you; continue to be my friend, as you will always find me yours."

LUDWIG VAN BEETHOVEN

I don't mind going nowhere as long as you're with me.

Our friendship isn't a big thing; it's a million little things.

You are the best sort of life insurance.

I've never **quite** lost the **wonder** of the **companionship** that you **deliver**.

You'll still be here when I'm past my prime.

"Do not protect yourself by a fence, but rather by your friends."

CZECH PROVERB

We have so much in common, it's almost scary!

I will never forget the memories we have made, and I can't wait for the ones still to come.

We **may** have our **differences**, but we **always** end up **on top**.

"Similarities **create friendships** while differences **hold** them **together**."

ANON

The only time you get on my case is to help me pack.

We're never so far out of range that we can't shoot the breeze.

You're a foul-weather friend.

I stop hurrying when I'm with you.

"Truly great friends
are hard to find,
difficult to leave,
and impossible
to forget."

G. RANDOLF

You'll walk miles with me on the beach.

You remember my birthday and forget my age!

You'll always be my friend: You know too much!

Did you **know** that we **share** some of my **fondest memories**?

"Friendship is a meandering river whose course can never be diverted and whose current should not be hastened."

MARGARET POWELL

Every day you make it your job to be my friend. I hope you never retire!

You are like an old comfy chair that I never want to part with.

"My father always used to say that when you die, if you've got five real friends, then you've had a great life."

LEE IACOCCA

We're two of a kind.

You are **better** than a **pair** of **gloves**, because I do **not** have to **drag** you around with me for **you** to **keep** me **warm**.

Our friendship will never die—just get reorganized.

When you **phone** you
just have to say **"Hi"** and
I **know** it's **you**.

You are **worth** living **for**.

*It is always hard to
say good-bye, but let's
never say farewell.*

It is your tiny, everyday gifts that are so special: a kind word, a smile, the smallest act of caring.

Even though we **might** spend a **long** time apart, when we come **together** again there is **no** awkwardness.

You're the only
person I know
who comes with a
lifetime guarantee.

When we are long in the
tooth we'll sit together
and remember our youth.

"When we are young, friends are, like everything else, a matter of course. In the old days we know what it means to have them."

EDVARD HAGERUP GRIEG

You never ask
"What's in it for me?"

*Forgiveness is just one
of your habits.*

Wherever you go, you
go with all my heart.

*Choose to be alone or
choose instead to spend
your time with friends.
Time will pass regardless.*

In life you're interested
in the whole **story**,
not just your own
scenes.

You **help** me to **understand** my **past** and **shape** my **future**.

Every year, even though the leaves fall from the trees and the winter storms bring icy winds, I can always warm my heart in front of yours.

You are as dear to me as
my own fingers—when
things get too difficult,
I can always count on you.

When **tomorrow** starts
without you, you'll
always be in my thoughts
and your **memory** will
live on in my **heart.**

We **laugh** so much **together** that when we get **old** we can be sure our **wrinkles** will be in the **right** places.

"Treat your friend as a spectacle."

RALPH WALDO EMERSON

The thought of all the yesterdays we have shared makes me look forward to all the tomorrows we will share and reminds me to make the most of every special day we spend together.

When **everyone else** was **kissing** my **feet**, you gently held my **hand**.

You have shown me how to replace blind satisfaction with a little true happiness.

You are there through **ups** and **downs**, **smiles** and **frowns**.

If I could change the past, I would change many things, but you would play exactly the same part.

"*With clothes the new are best; with friends the old are best.*"

CHINESE PROVERB

Thanks for letting me be more human.

We will be **friends**
until **forever**,
just you **watch**.

*You will seek me out
even in heaven.*

You're open all hours.

"True friendship is like sound health; the value of it is seldom known until it be lost."

CHARLES CALEB COLTON

I may **not** remember **exactly** what you **did** or what you **said**, but I will **always** remember **how** you made me **feel**.

Friendship exists for the deepening of the spirit.

Even when we don't talk, your heart still listens.

Even when I try to push you away, you keep coming back.

We have infinite faith in one another.

A friend gives help and comfort before advice.

You are like my **second** family, only **closer**.

"Friendship is the only cement that will ever hold the world together."

WOODROW WILSON

Some **friends** help me to move **house**. **You** help me to move **mountains**.

When I see the world through your eyes, my mind is filled with outrageous possibilities.

Together we can do so much more.

Between now and our destinies, I know you'll be here.

Thanks for inviting me over to the sunny side of the street.

I can **depend** on you to be **there** when the **good** times **aren't**.

Even if we're **all** on a **road** to **nowhere,** let's meet up for a **coffee** at the **end.**

"I have no talent for making new friends but, oh, such genius for fidelity to old ones."

DAPHNE DU MAURIER

The best thing is,
you already know
all the reasons
why we are friends.

Published by MQ Publications Limited
12 The Ivories
6–8 Northampton Street
London, N1 2HY
email: mqpublications.com
website: www.mqpublications.com

Copyright © 2003 MQ Publications Limited
Text copyright © 2003 Michael Powell

Editor: Karen Ball
Design concept: Balley Design Associates
Design: Philippa Jarvis

ISBN: 1-84072-534-6

10 9 8 7 6 5 4 3 2 1

Printed and bound in China